My Daughter, Jo
My Special Friend

Written by Roy Honegger
Cover Design and Typography by
Roy Honegger and Dmitry Feygin

Published by Great Quotations Publishing Co.,
Glendale Heights, IL

Library of Congress Catalog Card Number: 97-078976

ISBN 1-56245-280-0

Printed in Hong Kong

Every generation must go further than the last,
or what's the use in it?

—Meridel Le Sueur

The bond between women is a circle—
we are together within it.

—Judy Graham

The little things that I never really noticed all come back now as I have my own daughter. Thanks, Mom, for being such a strong model for me. You made it seem so easy.

—Meredith Ralston

Trouble is, kids feel they have to shock their elders and each generation grows up into something harder to shock.

—Cal Craig

I believe many have forgotten the value of characteristics and activities which identify the family as unique and different. They are called "traditions."

—Dr. James Dobson

To My Daughter
There are so many things I try to say.
While you half listen, lost in your own dreams.
I want to point out pitfalls, smooth your way,
for love is not all roses and moonbeams.
Yet as I sigh, I suddenly recall, and see
that you are all alike, and all.
As middle age grows too I'm discerning.
That half the joy of love is in the learning.

—*Virginia Shearer Hopper*

Family life is the source of the greatest human happiness.

—Robert J. Gavinghurst

Never grow a wishbone, daughter,
where your backbone ought to be.

—Clementine Paddleford

Life consists not simply in what heredity and environment do to us but in what we make out of what they do to us.

—Harry Emerson Fosdick

11

Look for the good, not the evil, in the conduct of members of the family.

—Jewish Proverb

*To forget one's ancestors is to be a brook without a source,
a tree without a root.*

—Chinese Proverb

For a wife, take the daughter of a good mother.

—Thomas Fuller

Mother to Daughter:
Darling, life is not in my hands…
I cannot promise very much…
I promise you love. Time will not take away that.

—Anne Sexton

A son is a son till he gets him a wife, but a daughter's a daughter all her life.

—Unknown

16

I fear, as any daughter would, losing myself back into the mother.

—Kim Chernin

Our first mother-daughter outing:
For three hours, knitting our thoughts and lives together
like old college roommates going toward a reunion.

—Phyllis Theroux

*Ancestral habits of mind can be constricting;
they also confer one's individuality.*

—Bharati Mukherjee

Traveling in the company of those we love is home in motion.

—Leigh Hunt

Mother to Daughter:
I am giving you the dark birds of the night, yes
they are mine, they are mine to give.

—Michele Murray

I've always believed that one woman's success
can only help another's success.

—*Gloria Vanderbilt*

Ideals and principles continue from generation to generation only when they are built into the hearts of children as they grow up.

—George S. Benson

One is not born a woman—one becomes one.

—Simone De Beauvoir

Our ancestors dwell in the attics of our brains as they do in the spiraling chains of knowledge hidden in every cell of our bodies.

—*Shirley Abbott*

There must always be a struggle between a mother and a daughter, while one aims at power the other at independence.

—*Unknown*

I happen to feel that total separation between parents and (adult) children is one of the great tragedies of our culture. Both generations really need the sustenance the other has to give.

—Adelaide Bry

Do not become paralyzed and enchained by the set patterns which have been woven of old. Build from your own feeling, your own thought and your own perception and help to further that beauty which has grown from the roots of tradition.

—Lotte Lehmann

It is not that I belong to the past, but that the past belongs to me.

—Mary Antin

We thought we were running away from the grownups,
and now we are the grownups.

—Margaret Atwood

Families are the most beautiful things in all the world.

—Louisa May Alcott

Every generation goes someplace bigger.

—Faith Sullivan

There is no hope or joy except in human relations.

—Antoine de Saint-Exupery

The older daughter is married off by her parents,
the younger daughter by her sister.

—Russian Proverb

Our children are not going to be just our children—they are going to be other people's husbands and wives and the parents of our grandchildren.

—*Mary S. Calderone*

Some of the older generation's criticism of the younger generation is heavily tinged with envy.

—*Unknown*

Daughters—
Advice from your mother comes naturally, after all she has been
where you are to follow.

—Unknown

Let us take our proper station;
We, the rising generation,
Let us stamp the age as ours!

—Mary Howitt

The conflict between generations results from a breakdown in mutual respect, and it bears many painful consequences.

—Dr. James Dobson

From Generation to Generation:
We should so live and labor in our time that that which came to us as
a seed may go to the next generation as blossom, and that which
comes to us as blossoms may go to them as fruit.

—Henry Ward Beecher

The ache for home lives in all of us, the safe place where we can go as we are and not be questioned.

—Maya Angelou

Daughters who despise their mothers do so until about age thirty when suddenly they become just like them.

—Unknown

One of the closest bonds a mother can have with her daughter comes through comforting.

—Unknown

43

The finest inheritance you can give a child is to allow it to make its own way, completely on its own feet.

—Isadora Duncan

But what mother and daughter understand each other, or even have the sympathy for each other's lack of understanding?

—Maya Angelou

Watching Clementine grow is one of the great satisfactions of my life. The center of the universe shifting from myself to another person is a great relief. It gives me the chance to give to another person. I'm not so concerned about my own life as I was before.

—Cybil Shepherd

Our affections are our life. We live by them; they supply our warmth.

—William Ellery Charming

There are only two lasting bequests we can hope to give our children. One of these is roots, the other, wings.

—*Hodding Carter*

Mother to Daughter:
I long to put the experience of fifty years at once into your young lives,
to give you at once the key of that treasure chamber every gem of
which has cost me tears and struggles and prayers, but you must work
for these inward treasures yourselves.

—Harriet Beecher Stowe

Intimacies between women often go backwards, beginning in revelations and ending up in small talk without loss of esteem.

—Elizabeth Bowen

Your relationships with people begin in the home, where you learn values. It's the responsibility of the family.

—Melba Moore

The woman who bore me is no longer alive but I seem to be her daughter in increasingly profound ways.

—Johnetta B. Cole

Mommy herself has told us that she looked upon us more as her friends than her daughters. Now that is all very fine, but still a friend can't take a mother's place. I need my mother as an example which I can follow, I want to be able to respect her.

—Anne Frank

When I stopped seeing my mother with the eyes of a child,
I saw the woman who helped me give birth to myself.

—Nancy Friday

Some people are your relatives but others are your ancestors,
and you choose the ones you want to have as ancestors.
You create yourself out of those values.

—Ralph Ellison

When we were children, we used to think that when we were grown-up we would no longer be vulnerable. But to grow up is to accept vulnerability.

—Madeleine L'Engle

A beautiful woman appeals to the eye; a good woman appeals to the heart. One is a jewel, the other a treasure.

—Napoleon Bonaparte

The relationship between a grandmother and granddaughter is a special relationship. It's teaching, telling, giving and bonding. It's learning family histories and traditions, things that have been passed from generation to generation. It's love shared.

—Francine Haskins

A family ought to have an identity that gives each member a sense of belonging.

—Dr. James Dobson

*Traditions are the guideposts driven deep into our subconscious minds.
The most powerful ones are those we can't even describe,
aren't even aware of.*

—Ellen Goodman

*It's not the flesh and blood, but the heart that
makes us mothers and daughters.*

—Anonymous

*In the woman's keeping is committed the destiny of
the generations to come after them.*

—Theodore Roosevelt

Mothers of daughters are daughters of mothers and have remained so,
in circles joined to circles, since time began.

—Signe Hammer

Don't try to be such a perfect girl, darling. Do the best you can without too much anxiety or strain.

—Jess Barnard

What I wanted most for my daughter was that she be able to soar confidently in her own sky, wherever that might be, and if there was space for me as well I would, indeed, have reaped what I had tried to sow.

—Helen Claes

The daughter tends to resent her mother as most people resent the imposers of rules, but even more so because there are more rules for daughters than for sons.

—Paula Caplan

All women become like their mothers. That is their tragedy.
No man does. That's his.

—*Oscar Wilde*

From the very beginning, the mother has to encourage the daughter to be her own person, not just let her go but encourage her!

—Nancy Friday

I'd rather see you poor men's wives, if you were happy, beloved, contented, than queens on thrones, without self-respect and peace.

—Louisa May Alcott

A perplexing and ticklish possession is a daughter.

—*Thomas Hardy*

The thoughts of a daughter are a kind of memorial.

—Enid Bagnold

A fluent tongue is the only thing a mother doesn't like her daughter to resemble her in.

—Richard Brinsley Sheridan

My eleven-year-old daughter mopes around the house all day waiting for her breasts to grow.

—Bill Cosby

A father gives his daughter the sense of what her bargaining position with all men will be.

—Shirley Abbott

O young thing, your mother's lovely armful!
How sweet the fragrance of your body!

—*Euripides*

Thou art thy mother's glass, and she in thee
Calls back the lovely April of her prime.

—William Shakespeare

I often tell Melanie to talk with her kids about the time problems and her own guilty feelings. Try to help them understand if you're not with them it doesn't mean you don't love them. Not until Melanie had children did she say, "Mom, I understand."

—Tippi Hedren, mother of Melanie Griffith

We are all daughters of the present, with the potential to impact a new motherhood as well as a new womanhood. But regardless of the changes that occur…there always will be a unique tie between mother and daughter in our society.

—Phyllis Magrab

From the time she was born, until she was 15, I didn't know where I left off and she began. We were joined at the hip or the heart or the brain.

—Lee Grant

He that would the daughter win
Must with the mother first begin.

—English Proverb

The amicable loosening of the bond between daughter and mother is one of the most difficult tasks of education.

—Alice Balint

It is hard to raise sons; and much harder to raise daughters.

—Sholem Aleichem

A good daughter is like a good piece of writing: candid, lyrical, graceful, moving, alive. I have seen a young girl walk across a room, intent on her intense errand, and it was like seeing a voice become visible, as if not her tongue but her motion said, "I will do this for my life."

—Paul Engle

I am a reflection of my mother's secret poetry as well as of her hidden angers.

—Audre Lorde

The mother should teach her daughter above all things to know herself.

—C. E. Sargent

Many a man wishes he were strong enough to tear a telephone book in half—especially if he has a teenage daughter.

—Guy Lombardo

You bring up your girls as if they were meant for sideboard ornaments; and then you complain of their frivolity.

—*John Ruskin*

A daughter is a treasure—and a cause of sleeplessness

—Ben Sirach

Mother to Daughter:
I know you know the value, the potential of what I've tried in my small way to write…maybe the spirit of the poems will go on past both of us, and one or two will be remembered in a hundred years.

—Anne Sexton

I have heard daughters say that they do not love their mothers.
I have never heard a mother say she does not love her daughter.

—Nancy Friday

There is an important line between mother and daughter, and mother and friend.

—Phyllis Magrab

So I took my daughter in my arms and said, "I love you."
I told her that she was precious to me, and I stroked her hair.
She sucked her thumb and lay there like a contented cat.

—Nikki Gerrard

How are we to be the mothers we want our daughters to have, if we are still sorting out who our own mothers are and what they mean to us?

—Letty Cottin Pogrebin

Say the word "daughter," slowly, prolong its gentle sound.
Notice the way it lingers on the tongue like a piece of candy.

—Paul Engle

The times we spent together took on a special intimacy, a quality that I remember best from the day I woke up and my daughter was brought to me in the hospital. I won't top that feeling in my lifetime.

—Tammy Grimes

From birth to age 18 a girl needs good parents. From 18 to 35 she needs good looks. From 35 to 55 she needs a good personality. From 55 on, she needs good cash.

—Sophie Tucker

She must not swing her arms as though they were dangling ropes; she must not switch herself this way and that; she must not shout; and she must not, while wearing her bridal veil, smoke a cigarette.

—Emily Post

A daughter living out a mother's thwarted ambition is a cause of fulfillment and envy to the mother, has a sense of the "mission" of her heritage and a terrible feeling of pressure. Such daughters have never felt free to fail.

—Louise Bernikow

*I stopped wearing jewelry long ago, once I realized
my children are what make me beautiful.*

—Carolyn Caton

The family—that dear octopus from whose tentacles we never quite escape, nor, in our inmost hearts, ever quite wish to.

—Dodie Smith

The family is one of nature's masterpieces.

—George Santayana

*When you look at your life, the greatest happinesses
are family happinesses.*

—Dr. Joyce Brothers

What feeling is so nice as a child's hand in yours? So small, so soft and warm, like a kitten huddling in the shelter of your clasp.

—Marjorie Holmes

In the effort to give good and comforting answers to the young questioners whom we love, we very often arrive at good and comforting answers for ourselves.

—Ruth Goode

Once the children were in the house the air became more vivid and more heated; every object in the house grew more alive.

—Mary Gordon

Is nothing in life ever straight and clear, the way children see it?

—Rosie Thomas

Family jokes, though rightly cursed by strangers,
are the bond that keeps most families alive.

—Stella Benson

See into life—don't just look at it.

—Anne Baxter

Mistakes are part of the dues one pays for a full life.

—Sophia Loren

In every child who is born, under no matter what circumstances, and of no matter what parents, the potentiality of the human race is born again.

—James Agee

Children ask better questions than do adults. "May I have a cookie?"
"Why is the sky blue?" and "What does a cow say?" are far more
likely to elicit a cheerful response than "Where's your manuscript?"
"Why haven't you called?" and "Who's your lawyer?"

—Fran Lebowitz

There was a little girl
Who had a little curl
Right in the middle of her forehead,
And when she was good
She was very, very good
But when she was bad she was horrid.

—Henry Wadsworth Longfellow

I want to have children while my parents are still young enough to take care of them.

—Rita Rudner

113

There are no ideal mothers, nor are there ideal daughters. Tension is intrinsic in the mother-daughter relationship and conflict is unavoidable.

—Phyllis Magrab

Because the "Perfect Mother" images exist, daughters feel guilty
for not regarding their mothers as perfect; but if they don't,
a whole culture out there is ready to pounce,
to encourage them to see her as a miserable failure.

—Paula Caplan

*What the mother sings to the cradle goes all the way down
to the coffin.*

—Henry Ward Beecher

Our child will not be raised in tissue paper!
We don't want her to even hear the word princess.

—*Juliana,*
Princess of the Netherlands

She is now only a few months old and at the beginning of it all, rolling her eyes for the first time at the world. A dangerous temptation for any father, new to the charms and vanities of parenthood, to use her as a glass in which to adore his own image, to act miracles and be a god again.

—Laurie Lee

If we step outside socially imposed injunctions, then…daughters and their mothers wield powers for one another's help as well as harm. They may even make of one another revolutionaries.

—Nancy Mairs

119

A daughter looking at her mother's life is looking at her own, shaping and fitting one life to suit the needs of another. Some have shaped monsters and some angels. Most who make angels see their mother as the sources of art, the tree of creative life.

—Louise Bernikow

The daughter begins to bloom before the mother can be content to fade, and neither can forbear to wish for the absence of the other.

—Samuel Johnson

She was a beautiful baby. She blew shining bubbles of sound. She loved motion, loved light…She was a miracle to me, but when she was eight months old I had to leave her daytimes with the woman downstairs to whom she was no miracle at all.

—Tillie Olsen

My love for her and my hate for her are so bafflingly intertwined that I can hardly see her. I never know who is who. She is me and I am she and we're all together.

—Erica Jong

So now you're eighteen and I'm all out of child daughters....
But there's no use sulking about it, I guess, and I might as well
try to make the best of it and welcome you into the ranks of the adult.
I'm sure you'll like our little club.

—Dashiell Hammett

I'm still wondering whether you're a person or not. We are two strangers tied to the same destiny, two beings united in the same body, unknown to each other, distant.

—Oriana Fallaci,
Letter to a Child Never Born

Until you make peace with who you are,
you'll never be content with what you have.

—Doris Mortman

*I watched you with the man whose life you will soon be sharing and
I was suddenly reminded of the play-weddings of your childhood.
And I thought of all the joys you have brought into my life since
I carried you under my heart.*

—Barbara Burrow

Yes, she is a nerve-wracking nuisance, just a noisy bundle of mischief. But when your dreams tumble down and the world is a mess—when it seems you are pretty much of a fool after all—she can make you a king when she climbs on your knee and whispers, "I love you best of all!"

—Alan Beck

Call it a clan, call it a network, call it a tribe, call it a family.
Whatever you call it, whoever you are, you need one.

—Jane Howard

Family life! The United Nations is child's play compared to the tugs and splits and need to understand and forgive in any family.

—May Sarton

Keep true to the dreams of thy youth.

—Johann Friedrich von Schiller

Starting as a secretary is a shrewd course for any ambitious young woman. It plugs you in at a higher level than most entry-level jobs. You can eavesdrop and learn a lot.

—Joan Manley

Some of us are becoming the men we want to marry.

—Gloria Steinhem

It's taken me all my life to understand that it is not necessary to understand everything.

—Rene Coty

I have found the best way to give advice to your children is to find out what they want and then advise them not to do it.

—Harry Truman

Develop your eccentricities when you are young. That way, when you are old people won't think you are going ga-ga.

—David Ogilvy

*A kiss can be a comma, a question mark or an exclamation point.
That's a basic spelling that every woman should know.*

—Mistin Guett

Whatever you may look like, marry a man your own age—
as your beauty fades, so will his eyesight.

—Phyllis Diller

A little bit of perfume doesn't hurt if you don't drink it.

—Darrell Royal

Home is not where you live but where they understand you.

—Christian Morgenstern

Your dresses should be tight enough to show you're a woman and loose enough to show you're a lady.

—Edith Head

Flops are a part of life's menu and I'm never a girl to miss out on any of the courses.

—Rosalind Russell

*I've dreamt in my life dreams that have stayed with me ever after,
and changed my ideas; they've gone through and through me,
like wind through water, and altered the color of my mind.*

—Emily Bronte

143

A mode of conduct, a standard of courage, discipline, fortitude and integrity can do a great deal to make a woman beautiful.

—Jacqueline Bisset

Like a round loaf, I kneaded you, patted you,
greased you smooth, floured you.

—Judith Toth

Heirlooms we don't have in our family. But stories we've got.

—Rose Chernin

A lady is one who never shows her underwear unintentionally.

—Lillian Day

Whatever women do they must do twice as well as men to be thought half as good. Luckily, this is not difficult.

—Charlotte Whitton

What families have in common the world around is that they are the place where people learn who they are and how to be that way.

—Jean Illsley Clarke

It's important to let people know what you stand for.
It's equally important to let them know what you won't stand for.

—B. Bader

I can govern the United States or I can govern my daughter Alice, but I can't do both.

—Theodore Roosevelt

How do you know when the fruit is ripe? Simple—
when it leaves the branch.

—Andre Gide

Never lend your car to anyone to whom you have given birth.

—Erma Bombeck

If a child lives with approval, he learns to live with himself.

—Dorothy Noble

You may give them your love but not your thoughts, for they have their own thoughts. You may house their bodies but not their souls for their souls dwell in the house of tomorrow, which you cannot visit, not even in your dreams.

—Kahlil Gibran

Go out into the world, find work that you love, learn from your mistakes and work hard to make a difference.

—Maurice R. Greenberg

Life would give her everything of consequence. Life would shape her; not we. All we were good for was to make the introductions.

—Helen Hayes

The thing that impresses me the most about America
is the way parents obey their children.

—Duke of Windsor

One of the few advantages to not being beautiful is that one usually gets better-looking as one gets older; I am, in fact, at this very moment gaining my looks.

—Nora Ephron

To grown people a girl of fifteen and a half is a child still; to herself she is very old and very real; more real, perhaps, than ever before or after.

—Margaret Widdemer

A woman can be both moral and exciting—
if she also looks as if it was quite a struggle.

—Edna Ferber

In those days, people did not think it was important for girls to read.
Some people thought much reading gave girls brain fever.

—*Ann McGovern*

Childhood is a prison sentence of twenty-one years.

—Thomas Szasz

My father had always said that there are four things a child needs—
plenty of love, nourishing food, regular sleep and lots of soap and
water—and after those, what he needs most is some intelligent neglect.

—Ivy Baker Priest

Nature makes boys and girls lovely to look upon so they can be tolerated until they acquire some sense.

—William Lyon Phelps

Where are you going, my little one, little one,
Where are you going, my baby, my own?
Turn around and you're two,
Turn around and you're four,
Turn around and you're a young girl going out of my door.

—Malvina Reynolds

Misery is when you make your bed and then your mother tells you it's the day she's changing the sheets.

—Suzanne Heller

Other Titles By Great Quotations

201 Best Things Ever Said
The ABC's of Parenting
As a Cat Thinketh
The Best of Friends
The Birthday Astrologer
Chicken Soup & Other Yiddish Say
Cornerstones of Success
Don't Deliberate ... Litigate!
Fantastic Father, Dependable Dad
Global Wisdom
Golden Years, Golden Words
Grandma, I Love You
Growing up in Toyland
Happiness is Found Along The Way
Hollywords
Hooked on Golf
In Celebration of Women
Inspirations Compelling Food for Thought
I'm Not Over the Hill
Let's Talk Decorating
Life's Lessons
Life's Simple Pleasures
A Light Heart Lives Long
Money for Nothing, Tips for Free

Mother, I Love You
Motivating Quotes for Motivated People
Mrs. Aesop's Fables
Mrs. Murphy's Laws
Mrs. Webster's Dictionary
My Daughter, My Special Friend
Other Species
Parenting 101
Reflections
Romantic Rhapsody
The Secret Language of Men
The Secret Language of Women
Some Things Never Change
The Sports Page
Sports Widow
Stress or Sanity
Teacher is Better than Two Books
Teenage of Insanity
Thanks from the Heart
Things You'll Learn if You Live Long Enough
Wedding Wonders
Working Women's World
Interior Design for Idiots
Dear Mr. President

GREAT QUOTATIONS PUBLISHING COMPANY
1967 Quincy Court
Glendale Heights, IL 60139 - 2045
Phone (630) 582-2800
Fax (630) 582- 2813